A HISTORY OF FIREARMS

*Deringer single-shot
percussion pistol*

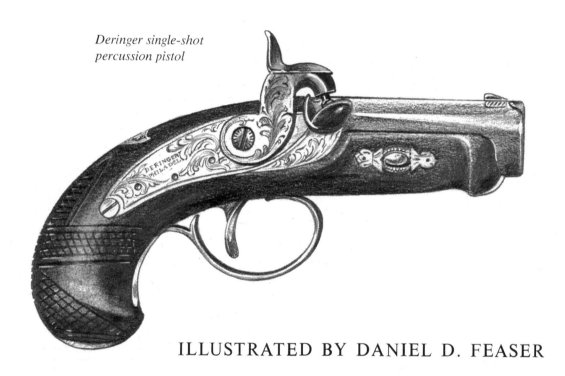

ILLUSTRATED BY DANIEL D. FEASER

A HISTORY
OF FIREARMS

HAROLD L. PETERSON

CHARLES SCRIBNER'S SONS   *NEW YORK*

The Company of Military Collectors & Historians through its Reviewing Board takes pride in sponsoring this book as a popular, responsible work in weapons history for younger readers.

HENRY I. SHAW, JR.
Editor in Chief, CMC&H

Reviewing Board
CHARLES E. HANSON, JR.
C. MEADE PATTERSON
HERMANN W. WILLIAMS, JR.

ALMOST SEVEN HUNDRED YEARS AGO the first gun was fired. Ever since, men have worked to improve guns, to make them shoot farther, faster and more accurately—and to make them simpler and more foolproof. Many men, some famous and some unknown, have contributed their genius to the development of firearms: men like astronomer and clockmaker Marin le Bourgeoys, soldier Patrick Ferguson, clergyman Alexander John Forsyth, shirtmaker Oliver Winchester, and skilled gunsmiths Christian Sharps and Samuel Colt. Through their efforts guns have evolved from crude tubes fired by a lighted coal or a red-hot iron to the smoothly accurate multi-shot weapons of today. In the process they have also played an important part in shaping the history of the world.

CONTENTS

THE INVENTION OF GUNPOWDER as a means of hurling a projectile brought with it a whole new era, not only in the development of weapons but also to all of history. Man had been on earth for almost a million years before he made this discovery. During all that time physical strength had been the basis of power. The strongest man could hurl a spear farthest and hardest, bend the most powerful bow, and deal the heaviest strokes with his sword or ax. This gave him mastery in battle and control of his fellow men. With the coming of firearms, size and strength lost their importance. A small man with a gun was just as powerful as a big one.

THE ORIGIN
OF
FIREARMS

9

No one knows just when or where gunpowder was first discovered. There were many stories about its invention in remote antiquity by the Chinese, the Arabs, and the Hindus, but recently these have been challenged. It now seems that the explosive mixture containing charcoal, sulphur and salt-peter, was gradually developed in western Europe between 1225 and 1250 where the formula was recorded by several monks. One of them, Roger Bacon, considered the new discovery so dangerous that he wrote the description and formula in a secret code for fear that it would fall into the wrong hands.

Even after the invention of gunpowder, it took about fifty more years before any one thought of using it to throw a projectile. Once again, no one knows who first thought of this, but there are records which show that some kinds of guns were in use by 1300 or very shortly thereafter.

The earliest picture of a gun that can be believed is dated 1326. It is in a manuscript written by Walter de Milemete to teach his pupil (who later became King Edward III of England) what the duties of a king were. The gun, or cannon, shown is a most unusual one, shaped like a vase. It is

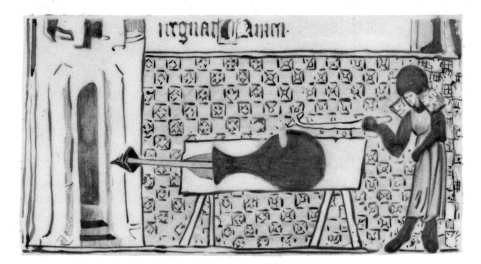

Earliest picture of a gun, from de Milemete manuscript

lying on a table, and an arrow-shaped projectile is shooting out its muzzle as a man in armor holds the red-hot wire he has just thrust into the powder to set it off. There is no way to tell what the cannon and the arrow were made of, but both were probably iron, including the "feathers" on the arrow.

About the same time, cannon of more usual shapes also appeared. These early cannon were made of many bars of iron welded together and then banded with hoops in much the same way as a wooden barrel. Some of the earliest ones were breechloaders with separate chambers that could be removed for loading. Otherwise they were simple tubes, closed at one end, and fastened to a huge beam that could be laid on the ground and propped up with stones or logs if they had to be aimed higher.

HAND CANNON

Portable guns that could be held and fired (small arms as they are called) first appeared about 1350. Since they were simply smaller versions of the big guns of the period, they have been given the name "hand cannon." As a rule, they were just tubes of iron or brass, like their bigger brothers, closed at one end and with a "touch hole" two inches or so from the closed end or "breech." They were fired by thrusting a red-hot wire through this hole into the powder in the "bore," as the inside of the barrel is called.

Aside from being smaller than the regular cannon, these hand cannon also differed in the way they were held and fired. Gun barrels become hot when they are fired, and after a number of shots a man can no longer hold the bare metal. He needs something to protect his hands. He also needs a lever to help control the recoil or "kick" when the gun goes off. A wooden stock met both these needs. The first stocks were long straight sticks. Sometimes they were inserted into a socket at the breech of the barrel; sometimes the barrel was fastened on top with metal bands.

Firing the hand cannon

As he prepared to fire such a hand cannon, the shooter clamped the stock between his left arm and body and steadied it with his left hand. Then he inserted the red-hot wire with his right hand. Larger guns were sometimes fired with the barrel supported by a forked rest and the butt of the stock braced in the ground. Still others required the services of two men, one to hold and one to insert the wire.

Improvements came rapidly in the next hundred years. The touch hole was moved from the top of the barrel to the right side, and a little cup or "pan" was placed under it. Additional powder could be put in this pan

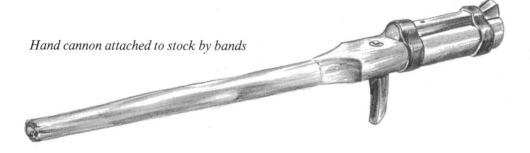

Hand cannon attached to stock by bands

Late hand cannon with socket for inserting the stock

Hand cannon with forged iron stock

so that the gun would be more sure to go off. Then a cover was added to protect this powder from the rain and dampness. The barrels were made longer, and the stocks were shortened and broadened.

The development of the pan made a big difference in the usefulness of the hand cannon. As long as the soldier needed a red-hot wire to fire his gun, he had to stay near a fire. With some powder exposed on the outside of the barrel, he could begin to use other means of touching it off. A glowing coal held in tongs offered him a little more freedom to move about. Then came the invention of "match."

Match was a lightly twisted rope of hemp which had been soaked in a solution of saltpeter and spirits of wine so that it would burn slowly and steadily, much like the modern punk. A moderate length of match would burn for hours if the weather was good, and the soldier with the lighted match in his hand could walk about wherever he pleased.

Next, an ingenious soul devised a way to fasten the match to the gun and keep it always in position. He did this with a simple S-shaped bar which was pivoted in the middle. He made a clamp on the upper end of this bar, or "serpentine" as it was called, and fastened the lighted match in it. With the match in place, all the shooter had to do was raise the lower end of the bar. The lighted match end would then be lowered automatically, bringing it into contact with the powder in the pan. It could all be done with the pressure of a finger. The right hand could now also be used for supporting the gun, thus relieving the pressure on the left hand. Even more important, the soldier no longer had to keep his eye on the end of the match as he touched it to the powder. Now he could look where he was shooting!

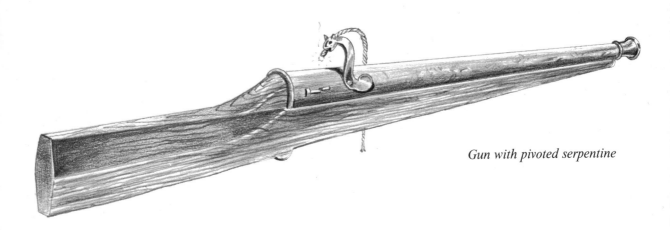

Gun with pivoted serpentine

Such crude firearms seem like relics of the far distant past. Yet it was just such guns that first came to America. In his journals, Columbus recorded that his landing party carried crossbows, a "Turkish" bow and "hand guns." This was October 1492, and for guns the next century was fateful indeed. The wilderness and unknown perils of the New World waited to be conquered by the new weapon at the same time that it was undergoing a period of rapid technical development.

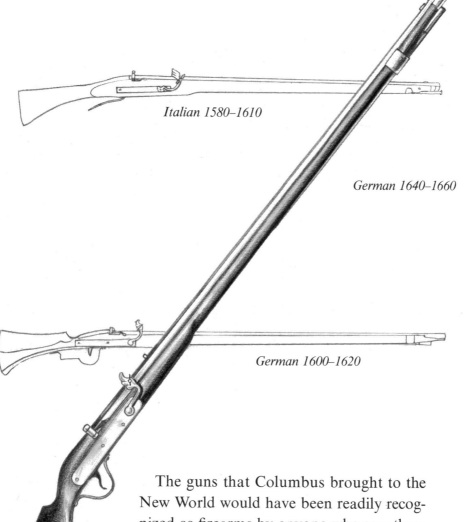

Italian 1580–1610

German 1640–1660

German 1600–1620

The guns that Columbus brought to the New World would have been readily recognized as firearms by anyone who saw them today. They had stocks, and they had barrels. The one essential thing they didn't have was a lock— that is, a mechanism for setting off the charge. It had either to be done with a lighted match held in the hand or clamped in a serpentine that was moved by the hand.

Just about the time that Columbus sailed from Spain the first real gun locks were coming into existence. A spring was made to act against the serpentine so that the end with the match would be held up away from the priming powder unless it was pushed down and held. Then a lever, the first trigger, was attached so that this pressure could be applied easily by the right hand as it steadied the gun. When the fingers squeezed the lever, the serpentine moved forward and touched the end of the match to the priming powder. When they relaxed, the serpentine moved back and carried the match away. All of the working parts except the serpentine were attached to the inside of a flat plate of metal called the lock plate and thus were protected from the weather.

Here was another major step forward, making the shooter's part easier and giving him a better hold on his weapon while he fired.

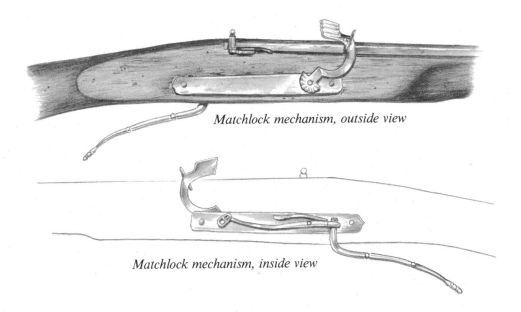

Matchlock mechanism, outside view

Matchlock mechanism, inside view

The matchlock was the basic military firearm in Europe for the next 200 years. During all that time there were only minor changes in its design. It was made lighter and easier to handle, and the long lever trigger was replaced by a shorter one which acted indirectly through another lever much like the trigger on a modern gun. Since this permitted a much smaller trigger, it could then be placed inside a trigger guard and so protected from bumps which might cause an accidental discharge.

This was the kind of gun that most of the early settlers brought to America. John Smith and the other colonists at Jamestown had them, as did the French settlers at Fort Caroline in Florida and the Pilgrims at Plymouth. The blunderbuss with its wide flaring muzzle which is shown in so many pictures of the Pilgrims, was unknown at the time. They really relied on the matchlock both for obtaining meat for their table and for protection against the Indians.

Despite its popularity, the matchlock had many disadvantages. The necessity for a lighted match was probably the worst. Friction matches such as we have today were unknown. Thus it was necessary to light the match at a fire any time it seemed likely that there would be need to shoot in the near future. Once it was lit, the match required constant adjustment so that enough stuck out from the jaws of the serpentine to reach the priming powder in the pan. If the match burned back to the serpentine, it would go out. Rain would put it out, rendering the gun useless, and so would a high wind. A lighted match was always a hazard in the presence of gunpowder, and its glow at night or even its smell in the daytime might prevent a successful surprise attack.

The settlers in America felt all of these drawbacks even more keenly than did the people of Europe. Over here, a man needed a gun constantly, and it had to work properly if he and his family were to survive. The English explorer Henry Hudson and his men were badly mauled by the Indians on the banks of his newly discovered river when a rainstorm put out the matches of his men without affecting the bowstrings of the Indians. On their famous march to discover the Mississippi River, Hernando de Soto's men complained that an Indian could shoot many times (and more accurately too) while a man with a matchlock shot only once. Something faster and surer was needed!

THE
WHEEL LOCK

*Operating the spanner
of the wheel lock*

The answer to these needs came in the form of an entirely new kind of gun—one that produced its own fire for igniting the priming. According to tradition this revolutionary arm was invented about 1517 by Johann Kiefuss, a German gunsmith working in Nuremberg, though there is some evidence it had actually been invented earlier. This device was called a wheel lock, and it worked much like the modern cigarette lighter. A piece of iron pyrite was clamped in a vise called a "dog head" and held against a rough-edged wheel which entered the priming pan and revolved when the trigger was pulled. This action produced a spark and so set off the charge. After each shot, the wheel was wound against a spring by a special wrench called a spanner. Then the gun could be loaded and primed and held ready for the next shot.

THE
WHEEL LOCK

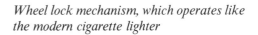

The wheel lock was a tremendous advance over the slow and cumbersome matchlock. The burning match with all its dangers and disadvantages could be left behind. The new gun could be carried ready for instant use, and it was much less apt to be affected by rain or wind.

Wheel lock mechanism, which operates like the modern cigarette lighter

The wheel lock made the pistol practical. Since both hands were required to manage the match, there had been no advantage in developing a light matchlock handgun. In later years matchlock pistols were made in the Orient, but almost none were made in Europe. With the wheel lock pistol, firearms became a suitable weapon for cavalry as well as infantry, and there were rapid changes in military tactics, especially in northern Europe.

The wheel lock did not immediately supersede the matchlock as a military weapon in Europe. Despite its superiority as a gun, it had some serious disadvantages. Its lock was a complicated mechanism, and therefore it cost more money. Also, the separate spanner was a drawback. It might get lost; and without the spanner, the gun was useless. Thus the wheel lock was used primarily for mounted troops who could not handle the matchlock, for elite organizations such as princely bodyguards where cost was of no importance, and for sporting or personal arms for those who could afford them.

THE
WHEEL LOCK

Arquebus

Pistol

Musket

THE
WHEEL LOCK

Cavalrymen with wheel lock pistols

In America the situation was quite different. Here a good dependable gun was more important to the average man, and conditions in the wilderness required an arm that could be fired quickly under all sorts of conditions. For these reasons, the wheel lock was more popular among average people in America than it was in Europe. If a man's life was apt to depend on his weapon, he did not worry as much about its cost. Parts of many wheel locks have been excavated by archeologists at the site of colonial Jamestown, the first permanent English settlement in America, and Samuel de Champlain undoubtedly used one in his famous fight with the Iroquois near Lake Champlain in 1609.

Many different names were applied to the early matchlocks and wheel locks. The most common ones probably were musket, arquebus and pistol. These terms meant different things at different times, but generally a pistol was a short gun designed to be held and fired with one hand. A musket was a heavy military arm designed to be fired from the shoulder. Sometimes it was so heavy that a forked rest was needed to help hold it while it was being aimed and fired. The arquebus was a lighter firearm than the musket but held with two hands and fired either from the shoulder or in front of the chest. It did not need a rest. Later the term was sometimes used to distinguish a wheel lock from a matchlock.

Still the inventors worked to improve the wheel lock, to simplify it and do away with its spanner. Within fifty years they succeeded. The new lock was simplicity itself, producing its spark by striking flint against steel in the same way the average householder of the time lit his fires. In the gun lock the flint was held in a vise on the end of a pivoted arm called the cock. The steel, also on a pivoted arm, was directly opposite the cock and right above the pan. When the trigger was pulled, a strong main spring swung the cock sharply forward so that the flint struck the steel a glancing blow and produced a shower of sparks which fell into the pan below.

This new system appeared over a period of years in several different parts of Europe, and so there were a number of variations of it. In the area that is now Holland and Belgium there was the snaphaunce. In Spain and Italy there was the miquelet. There was the Scandinavian "snaplock," the English lock, "dog" lock, and finally the "true" flintlock. All used the same principle of flint striking steel.

Most important was the flintlock, which quickly supplanted both the matchlock and the wheel lock and became the standard gun lock for most of Europe and America for more than 200 years. The inventor of the flintlock was probably Marin le Bourgeoys, gunmaker to King Louis XIII of France about 1610–1615, and a real genius in several fields. He combined

Flintlock operation, 1

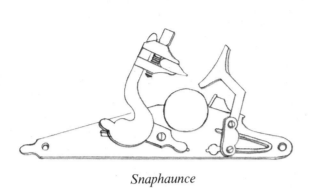

Snaphaunce

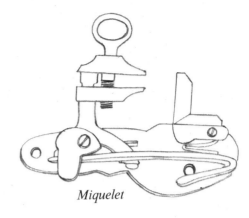

Miquelet

Flintlock

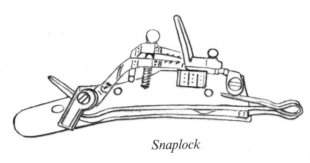

Snaplock

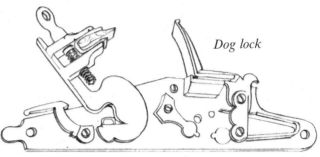

Dog lock

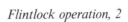

Flintlock operation, 2

Marin le Bourgeoys and one of his flintlocks

features of several of the earlier flint arms and produced a simple, safe and reliable gun. From France the new gun quickly spread throughout most of Western Europe, and by 1700 it was almost universally used. With this arm Americans conquered the wilderness west of the Alleghenies, fought in the French and Indian War, the Revolution, and the War of 1812. Some flintlocks even saw service during the Mexican War and the Civil War. All in all, flint arms were used during a far longer period of American history than any other type of firearm.

THE PERCUSSION CAP

Ever since the invention of the wheel lock in 1517, the whole theory of firing a gun had been based upon producing a spark by striking a stone (first iron pyrite, then flint) against steel. For almost 300 years gun locks were based on this principle. Then came an invention that changed things completely.

Flintlock operation, 3

The Reverend Alexander John Forsyth, a Scottish minister, discovered a chemical compound that would explode when it was struck a sharp blow. A keen sportsman as well as a student of chemistry in his spare hours, Forsyth quickly devised a way of applying his new invention to a gun. The exploding mixture, called a "percussion" compound because it went off when struck, could be placed in a tube leading to the inside or bore of a gun so that the sparks it produced would fire it. He made his first percussion lock in 1805 and obtained a patent in 1807.

Alexander John Forsyth and his "scent bottle" lock

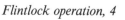

Flintlock operation, 4

Forsyth's invention was truly important. The separate priming powder that had to be put into the pan of all of the previous kinds of guns was no longer necessary. There were no longer any free sparks that might be dangerous. Weather could not affect the gun unless it was so wet that it damaged the charge inside the barrel. The new percussion primer was almost completely waterproof. This invention also was the basis for the later metallic cartridges which we use today. A whole new field of possibilities was opened up.

Once the percussion compound had been invented, it was still necessary to find the best way of using it. Forsyth's own lock used the compound in a loose powder which was poured out of a little container fastened to the lock plate. Because this container resembled a perfume bottle of the period, these locks have often been called "scent bottle" locks.

Other inventors tried other ways. The compound was molded into pellets and tubes, and the guns using them were called pill locks and tube locks. Then came the final form, the percussion cap.

Several men claimed the honor of inventing the percussion cap. The most likely one, however, was Joshua Shaw, an Englishman who was living in Philadelphia at the time. He applied for a United States patent, but was refused because he was not a citizen. Later his claims were recognized, and he was given a small sum of money to make up for what he had lost because he did not have a patent on the cap.

The percussion cap looked very much like the top hat of that day. The first ones were made of very thin iron. That was in 1814. Then came pewter, and, finally, in 1817, copper, the metal of which they are still made. Inside the cap, at the bottom of the cavity, a small amount of the percussion compound was placed and covered with a piece of tinfoil sealed with a drop of shellac to make it waterproof.

*Flintlock operation, 5
Step 6*

Percussion caps

In order to use the cap, it was placed over a tube which protruded from the breech of the gun barrel. This tube was called a nipple or a cone. The hammer of the gun, which acted very much like the cock of a flintlock, struck the cap a sharp blow. This set off the compound and produced a flash which followed the tube into the bore and fired the gun.

Despite the obvious advantages of the percussion cap, it took about 25 years for it to supplant the flintlock in Europe and America. Sportsmen were the first to turn to the new gun. Military men were slower. They had to be sure the new system was better in all ways.

RIFLING

A rifle is a gun with spiral grooves cut in the sides of the bore. These grooves make the bullet spin as it leaves the gun so that it will go straighter and strike harder. For many years this principle had been applied to arrows and bolts for crossbows by angling the feathers to make them spin in flight, and it was not surprising that someone should think of trying to do the same thing for bullets.

No one knows who this clever person was or even whether more than one thought of it independently. Successful rifling was developed, however, in Germany or Austria between 1450 and 1500. Some authorities claim the invention for Leipzig, while others assert it was discovered in Vienna. At any rate, the earliest known rifled firearm that can be dated with certainty belonged to the Emperor Maximilian I of Germany, and it

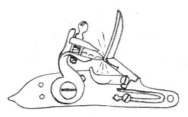

Flintlock operation, 7
Step 8

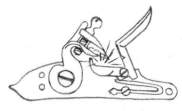

bears the coat of arms which he used between the years 1493 and 1508. It is a handsome gun with a bronze barrel and was originally a matchlock of some sort, but the lock is now missing. Maximilian was very much interested in arms and armor of all sorts and was often called the "Last of the Knights." A keen sportsman, he normally preferred to use the crossbow for hunting and referred to sporting firearms as "devilish fire guns" even though he approved of them as military weapons.

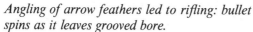
Angling of arrow feathers led to rifling: bullet spins as it leaves grooved bore.

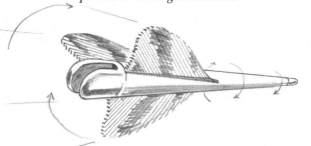

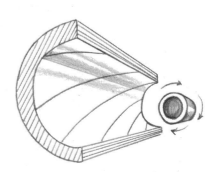

In order for a bullet to "take" the rifling and spin as it left the muzzle, it had to fit the bore tightly. There were two ways of doing this. In one, a ball the same size as the bore was forced down the barrel with repeated heavy blows from the ramrod. In the other, a smaller ball was wrapped in a greased patch of leather or cloth which would make it go down easier but still give a tight enough fit for it to take the rifling. Both of these methods were used almost from the beginning, and descriptions of them can be found in instruction books of the late 1500's.

No matter which one of these methods was used, the rifle was still much slower to load than the smoothbore in which the loose ball just dropped down the barrel. Sportsmen did not mind this delay if they could shoot more accurately, but military men did not like it. They wanted their troops to be able to shoot as fast as possible, and accuracy meant little since all the men were supposed to fire at once in a volley at a solid mass of enemy. Because of the force needed to push a tight-fitting bullet down a barrel, ramrods sometimes broke, and a gun with a broken ramrod was useless in battle. There were also other reasons which made the military men suspicious of the rifle. A man had to be more skilled to use one, and this was a drawback for anyone who had to drill raw recruits. Also, rifles cost more than smoothbores.

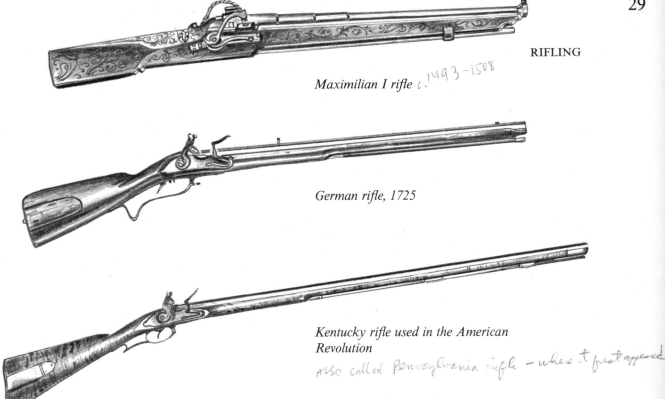

RIFLING

Maximilian I rifle c. 1493–1508

German rifle, 1725

Kentucky rifle used in the American Revolution

ALSO called Pennsylvania rifle – where it first appeared

For these reasons it was many years before the rifle was widely used to arm soldiers, but here and there some were issued. King Christian IV of Denmark was one of the first to provide them for some of his soldiers shortly after 1600. Others gradually did the same, and by the middle of the 1700's the use of the rifle for light troops and sharpshooters was widespread, especially in Germany and Scandinavia.

The usual European rifle was a short stubby gun with a large bore. Here in America, a very special and different rifle was developed to meet the frontier conditions. It is sometimes called the Pennsylvania rifle because that is where it first appeared, and sometimes the Kentucky rifle because it was so popular with the pioneers who settled in the territory that later became the states of Kentucky and Tennessee. This was the rifle of Daniel Boone, Daniel Morgan, the young Davy Crockett and many other American heroes of the frontier.

The Kentucky rifle developed directly from the short European rifle. Many of the early settlers of Pennsylvania came from Germany and

Kentucky rifle

Switzerland where the rifle was most popular. They brought their guns with them. Some of them were gunsmiths, and they made rifles here just as they had back home. Gradually, however, they began to change the design to make it more useful in their new land. They made the bore smaller so that less lead would be needed to make the bullets. Lead was sometimes scarce in the backwoods. They lengthened the barrel so that the gun would be more accurate at long distances. They used native American woods, particularly curly maple, for stocks, and they added a hinged brass cover to the box for the greased patches that was found in almost every rifle stock. Most of the European patch boxes had had sliding covers of wood or bone. When they finished with these changes they had produced a distinctly American gun, gracefully designed, and one of the most accurate the world had ever seen. It was America's first real contribution to firearms design—and it had been born from the needs of the frontier.

With the Kentucky rifle a trained marksman like Daniel Boone could perform feats of marksmanship that were astonishing. It was no trick at all for these men to hit a target the size of a man at 300 yards—and this was three times the effective range of a musket. There is a story of one company of men armed with these rifles in the American Revolution who put on a demonstration in which every man put a ball in a 7-inch target at a distance of 250 yards, and one marksman from Virginia put eight successive shots through a board 5 x 7 inches at 60 yards.

All along the frontier target shooting was as popular a sport as baseball is today. Every boy learned to handle a rifle expertly so that he could bring home game for the table and help protect his family from Indians if the need ever arose. This helped develop the tradition of marksmanship that is part of America's heritage. Even today Americans are expected to know more about

guns and how to shoot them than the average man from almost any other country.

The Kentucky rifle was an important gun in America's early wars. A few were used during the French and Indian War, and the British soldiers who saw them had some copies made for picked sharpshooters of their own. When the American Revolution broke out, after the battles of Concord and Lexington, the first troops to be raised for the new Continental Army commanded by George Washington were ten companies of riflemen from Pennsylvania, Virginia and Maryland. In the War of 1812, riflemen armed with Kentuckies again were prominent. Almost everyone has heard of their exploits at the battle of New Orleans under General Andrew Jackson where, together with superb American artillery, they turned back one of the best veteran armies of Europe, fresh from victories over Napoleon himself.

Despite its accuracy, the Kentucky rifle never became the standard arm for American soldiers in any war. It took too long to load with its patched ball, and it was not equipped with a bayonet. In the type of warfare used during the Revolution and the War of 1812, both speed in loading and the use of the bayonet were very important. Only once in a while did the Americans fight the British from behind trees and stone walls, as most stories tell. Usually they stood shoulder-to-shoulder in the open just as their opponents did.

Thus George Washington preferred the smooth-bored musket even if it was not as accurate, and most of the American soldiers carried them. He used his riflemen for special duties such as scouting and sharpshooting, and in those activities they performed most of their outstanding services.

If the rifle was to become a good military weapon as well as a fine hunting gun, some way had to be found to combine its accuracy with the speed and strength of the smoothbored musket. Gun designers from all over Europe and America set out to accomplish this.

First they tried to increase the speed of loading. Bullets had usually been round balls in the past, so at first they tried working with these. Then they tried different shapes until they finally found one that worked. It looked something like an upside-down ice cream cone with curved sides. This bullet could be dropped loosely down the barrel until it rested on top of the powder charge. When the powder went off, the gasses created by the explosion rushed up inside the hollow base of the bullet and spread the soft lead out to make it fit the barrel so tightly that it was forced into the rifling grooves at the same time that it was being shot out of the barrel.

Many men helped to develop this bullet. A Captain Norton and William Greener of England were followed by Captain C. E. Minié of France. Minié's bullet had an iron cup in its base which was driven forward by the force of the explosion to expand the lead. It was Minié who gave his name to all such expanding bullets, but it was actually an American who found that the iron cup was not needed and that if the bullet was properly designed, the gasses would spread the sides outward without it. James H. Burton, Assistant Master Armorer at the government's Harpers Ferry Armory, made this discovery in 1847. His new bullets were cheaper and easier to make and so were quickly adopted. Everyone called the new bullet "minie balls," but they were really Burton's.

Minié's bullet expanded by plug.

Burton's improved bullet expanded without plug. 1847

Now that they had a new quick-loading bullet, the United States set out to design guns to use it. In 1855 a pistol, a rifle, and a new sort of gun called a rifle musket, all using the new minie ball, were adopted by the Army. The rifle musket got its name because it was the same shape and size as a musket but had a rifled barrel instead of the old smooth one. Actually it was a rifle in every sense of the word, and shortly after the Civil War the distinction disappeared.

RIFLING

WAS THE RIFLE MUSKET THE MOST WIDELY USED GUN IN THE CIVIL WAR

While it lasted, however, the rifle musket played an important part in American history. It was the most widely used gun in the Civil War. Hundreds of thousands were used by both the Union and Confederate armies. It was an accurate gun, and a reasonably good marksman could be expected to hit a target six feet square at a distance of 500 yards, and at 1,000 yards he could hit a target eight feet square about half the time. It was a well–balanced arm. It had a bayonet. And with all its accuracy it could be loaded just as fast as the old musket.

The era of the smoothbore was over. Before the development of the minie ball and the rifle musket, most guns had been smoothbored. After the experiences of the Civil War, most guns were rifled. Only shotguns designed for small game and a few very specialized weapons were left without rifling.

The rifle of the Civil War period was as good a gun as any muzzle-loader could be. It was accurate, reasonably certain to go off, and it could be fired with fair rapidity. But it was still too slow to suit the men who had to use it. A good man could load, aim and fire such a gun in about 20 seconds under ideal conditions. Soldiers were expected to be able to shoot at least twice a minute in battle. If they could fire faster, they would have more chance of winning. And in hunting, a faster firing gun would mean more shots at the quarry before it disappeared. It would mean more assurance of enough meat for food and furs for clothing.

The muzzle-loader had another disadvantage, too. It took room to load one. A man normally had to stand up to pull out the ramrod and push the charge down the barrel. This meant that a soldier had to expose himself every time he reloaded and could not do it lying down or crouched behind a low bank or wall.

Guns that loaded at the breech and could shoot several times between loadings were needed to solve these problems of speed and ease. Almost from the beginning the desirability of such weapons had been recognized, and inventors had been trying to make guns that would do either or both of these things. During the early 1500's, for instance, when Henry VIII was King of England, a number of breech-loading matchlock pistols were

Henry VIII gun shield

made and fastened in the center of round shields of wood covered with metal. There were even little openings protected by bars right above the barrels for sighting the guns.

At the same time there were many other different attempts to produce breech-loading firearms. Some used little metal cylinders much like modern cartridge cases to hold the charges. Some had breeches which could be unscrewed or which were fastened with wedges. But all had serious drawbacks. They were easily broken. There were loose parts that could be lost. They tended to leak gas and flame from the explosion of the charge, and if they fit tightly, the fouling from the burned powder often made them so sticky that they would not work.

There were also many attempts at repeating arms, some breech-loading, some muzzle-loading. Sometimes these guns had a number of different barrels and locks all attached to the same stock and each holding one load. In other examples a revolving cylinder like that on a modern revolver was used. And some even had a whole series of charges loaded one on top of the other in a single barrel which were set off one after the other like a Roman candle. Once the shooter pulled the trigger he could not stop the firing until all the charges had been exploded. Needless to say, this last type was never very popular although it was tried both in Great Britain and America during the Revolution and the War of 1812.

One especially good early flintlock repeating breechloader was developed in Italy early in the 1600's. Michele Lorenzoni of Florence may have invented it. In this gun the powder and balls were loaded into separate holes or "magazines" in the stock. To load, the shooter simply pointed the gun muzzle up and turned a lever on the side backward, then pointed the gun down and turned the lever forward. This placed one ball and a charge of powder in the barrel and filled the pan with priming powder. It was all ready to shoot. The average gun of this "system Lorenzoni" was made to hold five, six, or seven shots in its magazines.

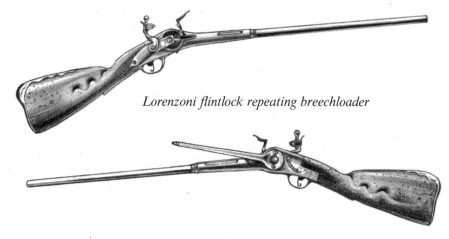

Lorenzoni flintlock repeating breechloader

The system Lorenzoni was excellent, but it was expensive to manufacture. Every part had to be made exactly right. If there was a loose fit or if the breech did not close perfectly, the flash from the explosion of the charge might set off the powder in the magazine in the stock and blow the gun to pieces with considerable danger to the shooter. Despite this disadvantage, such guns were made in Italy, England and elsewhere in Europe and probably also in America as well until almost 1800.

Farther north, Denmark developed a repeating rifle in which a turn of the trigger guard loaded and cocked the piece. The earliest known examples of this kind of rifle were made by Peter Kalthoff of Copenhagen about 1641, and so all such firearms are usually called Kalthoffs today. One very interesting fact about these rifles is that the Danish Foot Guards used some of them during the siege of Copenhagen in 1658–59 and during the Scanian War of 1675–79, and so they were probably the first repeating rifles ever used by regular troops in time of war.

Kalthoff's repeating wheel lock rifle

Shortly after these experiments with repeating firearms, single-shot breechloaders were also tried in various armies. France issued a few to selected units as early as 1723, and Austria armed its dragoons and light cavalry with breechloaders in 1770. Neither experiment lasted very long; and, generally speaking, the breechloader had to wait another hundred years before it came into its own.

But there was one early flintlock breech-loading rifle that is of especial interest to American history. In 1776 Patrick Ferguson, a British Army officer, perfected a rifle with a hole in the top of the breech that could be opened and closed by turning the trigger guard. One complete turn opened

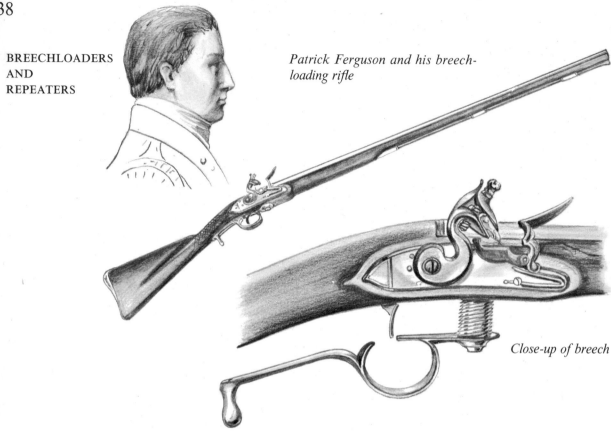

Patrick Ferguson and his breech-loading rifle

Close-up of breech

it so that a ball and powder could be dropped in. Then a turn in the opposite direction closed it, ready for cocking and priming. On June 1, 1776, Ferguson demonstrated his gun to a group of high officials by firing six shots a minute despite a heavy rain and performing other spectacular feats such as pouring a bottle of water into the barrel of the gun, thoroughly wetting all the powder, and then cleaning out the ruined charge and firing with a new one in less than half a minute. To top off his performance he hit the bull's eye while lying on his back on the wet ground.

No other gun had ever been able to do anything that could compare with this. But still the officials were not impressed, which was fortunate for the American Army. Only 100 or possibly 200 at most of these rifles were ever used during the War, and they went to Ferguson's own company of light infantry. When Ferguson was badly wounded at the battle of Brandywine, a year after his demonstration, the rifles were withdrawn from service and probably never used again. With great courage Ferguson continued his military career. The wound had shattered his right elbow, making that arm useless, but he taught himself to write, fence, and shoot left-handed and resumed active service with the army. He was killed at the battle of Kings Mountain in 1780 and is buried there on American soil. In his final battle he had none of his fine rifles to pit against the American Kentucky rifles that brought him down.

Because the British failed to accept the Ferguson rifle, the honor of becoming the first nation to adopt the breech-loading rifle as a standard military arm fell to the United States, in 1817. The inventor was John H. Hall of Portland, Maine, who had wanted to design ships. His first vessel promptly sank, however, and Hall then turned to guns. He not only invented a good breech-loading rifle but also designed the machinery for manufacturing it, and moved to Harpers Ferry to supervise the production of his guns at the United States Armory there. In doing this, Hall

Hall flintlock rifle

Breech of a percussion Hall

made manufacturing history. His were the first American firearms made on an assembly line system with completely interchangeable parts. This was one of the big steps that helped to move the United States forward as one of the world's leading industrial nations.

Hall's rifle was quite different from Ferguson's. Both were flintlocks, but Hall's had a section of the breech which was pivoted. It contained both the lock mechanism and the chamber—the rear part of the bore which holds the charge. To load, this section was tipped up, a charge was inserted, and then it was pressed back into place again and held there by a spring catch. It was a simple device, but it leaked gas and flame badly, and the little spur lever which operated the catch was apt to get caught in clothing or equipment or to hurt a soldier's shoulder as he carried it.

Despite these defects, Hall's rifles and shorter guns for cavalry, called carbines, were made for over 25 years. They were used all along the frontier, in minor wars with the Indians, in the Mexican War, and in the Civil War. Some of them were made as percussion locks as well as flintlocks, and the soldiers learned an interesting thing about the percussion Halls. They could take out the breech section and carry it in their pockets as a pistol in case of emergency. This helped to make the gun more popular with them, and during the Mexican War when a soldier on leave in a captured town was never completely safe, the breech from his Hall in his pocket made him feel much happier.

In Europe also, inventors continued to work toward a really satisfactory breechloader. In 1829 Johann Nicholas Dreyse invented a gun in which a long slender firing pin driven by the hammer passed all the way through the powder charge and exploded a cap seated at the base of the bullet which in turn set off the charge. Because of this long pin, the gun was quickly named the "needle gun," and the Prussian Army adopted it in 1841. Antoine Alphonse Chassepot of France developed a similar gun for his country, and Captain F. W. Scheel of Norway invented a tip-up breech

*Dreyse
needle gun*

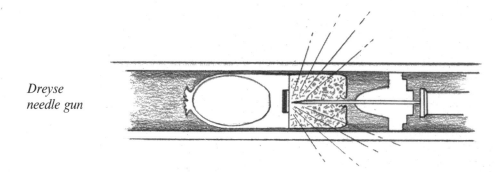

somewhat similar to the Hall that the Norwegian Army began to use in 1842. Still, there were problems. The long thin firing pin of the needle guns tended to break, and tip-up breeches leaked.

It remained for another American to come forward with the first really tight and strong action, in 1848. This man was Christian Sharps of Philadelphia, a young mechanic who had worked under John Hall at Harpers Ferry. Sharps' gun had a block which moved up and down in a slot at the breech of the gun. It was attached to the trigger guard in such a way that pulling outward on the guard dropped the block down and exposed the open breech end of the bore. A cartridge consisting of the bullet and a

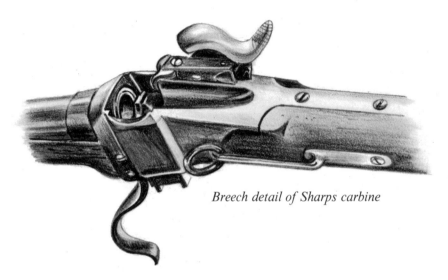

Breech detail of Sharps carbine

charge of powder wrapped in paper or linen could then be inserted into the bore. Pushing the trigger guard back into place raised the block, closing the breech and cutting off the end of the cartridge so that the powder would be exposed to the spark from the primer. The Sharps gun did not use percussion caps but had the same compound put in little discs which were automatically placed on the nipple as the hammer fell.

This new action met all the tests. It was simple and did not get out of order easily. It was so strong that even much too heavy loads would not bend or crack it. Even today the same basic idea is still used when great strength is needed.

The Sharps arrived on the scene just in time to take part in many great events in American history. The country was troubled over the issue of slavery, and there was open fighting in some sections. Reverend Henry

Ward Beecher suggested that a Sharps rifle carried more moral weight in the argument than a Bible, and the name "Beecher's Bibles" stuck. When John Brown raided the National Armory at Harpers Ferry, his men carried

*Sharps carbine
with coffee mill in stock*

Sharps carbines. They were widely used throughout the Civil War and were considered by the soldiers to be the best single-shot breechloader of the War. One special Sharps carbine even had a little mill in its stock for grinding the soldiers' coffee. Sharps arms played a large part in the winning of the West, and the famous Sharps buffalo gun helped provide food for many of the crews building the railroads across the continent.

Buffalo hunter spitting bullet into muzzle-loader (see page 35)

BREECHLOADERS
AND
REPEATERS

After the invention of the percussion system, it became possible to make real progress in the development of repeating arms, too. Success came first to the pistol makers with the pepperbox and then the true revolver.

A pepperbox pistol consisted of a number of separate barrels fastened together around a central axis so that they could be revolved. As each barrel passed under the hammer it could be fired. There was nothing new in the idea. Guns had been made on this principle for over 150 years. It was the percussion system that made them really practical at last. In the earliest pepperboxes the barrels had to be turned by hand. Then in 1836 Benjamin and Barton Darling of Massachusetts patented a pepperbox in which the barrels turned automatically when the hammer was cocked.

Pistols that had to be cocked by hand before the trigger could be pulled were called "single-action." Another Massachusetts gunsmith, Ethan Allen, improved upon that by inventing a pepperbox that was "double-action"—the hammer was raised automatically when the trigger was pulled. And the barrels revolved too. This was the pepperbox at its fullest development, the fastest firing gun of its time.

The Allen pepperboxes quickly became very popular. Householders welcomed them as protection against burglars. The forty-niners who

Pepperbox

swarmed to California to look for gold carried them across the plains in their covered wagons or on the long sea journey around the Horn. A few were even used by the cavalry in battle against the Indians, although they were small guns for military purposes.

Despite their speed, the pepperboxes were by no means perfect weapons. Their range was short, and the fact that the barrels were turning as the trigger was pulled made it impossible to aim accurately. Mark Twain, whose experience on the frontier and in mining camps made him familiar with the Allen, wrote many humorous comments about its lack of accuracy. In one, a man whose tall story about shooting a tree-climbing buffalo with his pepperbox had been doubted, complained, "I should have shot that long gangly lubber they called Hank if I could have done it without crippling six or seven other people—but of course I couldn't, the old Allen's so confounded comprehensive."

It was the revolver that solved the problem of accuracy and gradually replaced the pepperbox. The idea of the revolver was just as old as that of the pepperbox, but it took a shrewd Connecticut Yankee to refine it and make it work. Samuel Colt got the idea for his revolver at the age of sixteen when he shipped as a seaman on a voyage to India. On the long trip home in 1830 he whittled a model from wood. Then came the task of perfecting it and finally obtaining patents in 1835 and 1836. Colt's major improvement in revolver design was the automatic revolving of the cylinder when the hammer was cocked—and he obtained his patent on this feature just a few weeks before the Darling brothers got theirs on their pepperbox.

The revolver was better than the pepperbox in many ways. The fact that there was only one barrel which remained still while a cylinder holding the charges turned made it possible to aim accurately. Because only one barrel was necessary, revolvers were lighter and easier to carry, and so they could be made to fire larger bullets for greater distances.

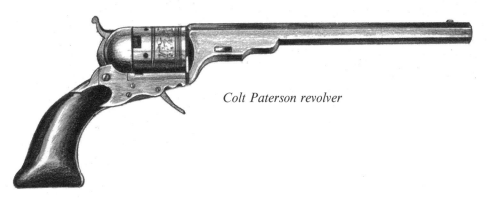

Colt Paterson revolver

These facts should have been apparent to anyone who wanted a gun, but still Colt had a very hard time getting started in business. His first factory at Paterson, New Jersey failed because he could not get enough orders for his guns, and Colt turned to other things. But some of his revolvers had found their way West, and there they began to win friends. In one instance, Captain Jack Hays and fifteen of his Texas Rangers armed with Colt Paterson revolvers defeated 75 Comanches in a surprise Indian battle. One of Hays' men, Samuel Walker, became a captain of dragoons in the United States Army, and with the help of many other soldiers who were impressed with the revolver he managed to obtain a government contract for Colt to make some of his guns for the Army. He also helped

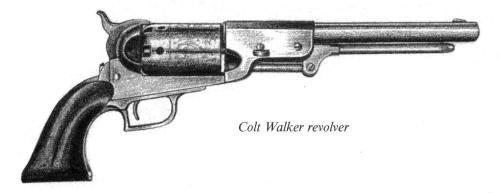

Colt Walker revolver

Colt redesign his pistol to improve it. This was the turning point in Colt's life. Orders now began to come in rapidly, and many different models were made for different purposes. The revolver was a success.

The Colt revolver was another of America's major contributions to the development of weapons, and it also greatly influenced the course of American history. The revolver was the ideal weapon for a mounted man. The West was just being opened up as the revolver came into being, and the men who conquered the wild territory, fought Indians and herded cattle did their work on horseback. It was a lawless period, too, because the country was growing too fast for organized law enforcement to keep up with it. Thus the outlaw, the sheriff and the peaceful citizen all carried revolvers. For fifty years the revolver was almost as much a part of a man's costume in that part of the country as his trousers. Then the growing period ceased; the Indians were pacified; the honest citizens were able to maintain law and order; and the revolver began to lose its importance except for policemen and soldiers.

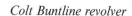

Colt Buntline revolver

In that fifty years, however, much happened to the revolver. Colt's original pistols were single-action and used percussion caps. Later metallic cartridges were used, and every boy is familiar with the famous Colt single-action "Peacemaker" of 1873, the great favorite both of the cowboys and the Army. A few of these, known as Buntline Specials, had extra long barrels. Wyatt Earp, the famous Marshall of Tombstone, carried a Buntline.

As soon as Colt's patent expired, many other companies began to make revolvers. The founders of one of these firms, Horace Smith and Daniel B. Wesson, even exceeded Colt in their contributions to the development of American weapons. Together these two friends invented a new repeating rifle and pistol using a new cartridge and laid the foundations for the later Winchester rifle. Really successful repeating rifles could not have been made without metallic cartridges which contained their own primer, and Smith and Wesson led the way in this field. They also pioneered in making revolvers which fired metallic cartridges, well before Colt.

The Winchester was not the only repeating rifle of its day, but it soon outdistanced all competition. The Spencer rifle, a seven-shot repeater which had been tested by Abraham Lincoln himself and had been a great favorite during the Civil War, came the closest, but after the war it dropped far behind and soon lost out completely. The quick-firing Winchester became the companion of the revolver for all work in the West: the revolver for close shooting, the rifle for long range. The Colt revolver and the Winchester were even made to take the same ammunition so that a cowboy needed to carry only one kind of cartridge.

With the Winchester, the Spencer, and the various other repeating arms of the world, it was necessary to eject the empty cartridge case, place another cartridge in the chamber and cock the gun between shots. This was done very quickly by moving a lever formed by the trigger guard in the case of the Winchester or by moving an arm backward and forward in the bolt action rifles.

The next step was the automatic or, more correctly, auto-loading weapon. These guns were developed late in the 1800's. Pistols and machine guns came first, followed more slowly by rifles. The first practical automatic pistol, the Schonberger, was manufactured in Austria in 1892. Within a few years there were many others. These new arms used the force of the recoil or the gasses released by the explosion of the charge to eject the empty cartridge case, load another from the magazine and cock the action. Later it became possible to make guns that were completely automatic and would keep firing as long as the trigger was squeezed and ammunition remained in the magazine. In modern terms, guns that must have their triggers squeezed for each shot are called semi-automatic while those that fire with a single squeeze are called full automatic. Automatic pistols were widely used during World War I, and during World War II many

BREECHLOADERS
AND
REPEATERS

Winchester rifle, model 1866

Sharps buffalo rifle

automatic arms appeared alongside the standard bolt-action rifles. By the time the war was over the automatic arm had become the standard military firearm throughout most of the world.

The M-14 rifle, adopted by the United States Army in 1957, can be fired as a semi-automatic or as a full automatic. Either way it will empty its 20-shot magazine in far less than the fifteen seconds it took the Revolutionary War soldier to load and fire his musket once.

M-14 rifle

As firearms improved, the ammunition with which they were fired also developed. In fact, it was often improvements in ammunition that permitted advances in firearms design. Three principal parts are found in almost all ammunition: the bullet, the powder for the charge, and, after Forsyth's experiments, the primer to set it off. Over the years there have been improvements in each of these elements and also in the means of carrying them and fastening them together.

The bullet is the simplest of the elements, but even that changed greatly. Early bullets were made of many materials, including stone, iron, bronze, tin, and even occasionally gold and silver. Lead also was used, and gradually its popularity increased until by 1600 it had superseded all the others. The shape of bullets changed too. In the beginning there were many different shapes. There were oval, triangular, diamond-shaped and barrel-shaped bullets, and some guns even fired little iron arrows. Eventually the round ball was found to shoot more accurately than the others, and it remained standard as long as smoothbored guns were used. When rifles became popular, the search for bullets that could be loaded quickly led to a variety of new shapes, including the expanding hollow-based minie ball. Then, with the appearance of the breechloaders, an expanding bullet was no longer needed. The cavity in the base was filled in, and the modern bullet gradually developed. As a final step, late in the 1800's, a method of covering the soft lead of the bullet with a thin skin of a harder metal was invented, and this was the beginning of the present-day jacketed bullet.

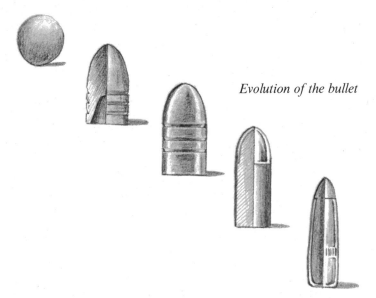

Evolution of the bullet

Gunpowder, too, made many advances. For most of the time since firearms were invented, they have been fired with black powder. This consisted of three main ingredients: sulphur, saltpeter and charcoal. At first these were just ground to a fine powder and mixed together. This was known as serpentine or meal powder. It would explode, but it was not very good. It had to be stirred frequently or the ingredients would settle out. It would absorb water from the atmosphere, and it left a lot of residue or fouling in the barrel of a gun after firing. By the middle of the 1500's it was found that most of these drawbacks could be overcome if the mixture was moistened with a little water or wine and forced through a sieve. This produced a powder made up of hard little grains, the size of the openings in the sieve, and for this reason it was called granulated or corned powder.

Black powder produced clouds of smoke.

Corned powder was a good, stable explosive, but it still had some defects. It gave off a quantity of white smoke, revealing the location of the shooter, and, in battle, sometimes completely filling the air so that neither side could see the other. Its explosive force was relatively low so that a large charge was needed, and it still left some residue to foul the gun.

The answer to these difficulties was finally found in smokeless powder. But this took several centuries. As early as the 1600's some chemists had experimented with different kinds of explosives, but they had been difficult to control and very violent. It was not until 1884 that a controllable explosive made with nitrocellulose was developed in France. Then another using nitroglycerine was invented by Alfred Nobel in Sweden a few years

Alfred Bernhard Nobel, inventor of smoke-less gunpowder—and philanthropist whose $9,200,000 bequest established the annual Nobel Prizes

later. In 1886 France adopted the new smokeless powder, and other countries soon followed her example. Some United States soldiers were still using black powder during the Spanish-American War, but by 1900 smokeless powder was in almost universal use for military arms. In sporting guns the change-over was slower.

Most improvements, however, came in the methods of carrying and using the ammunition. In the beginning, powder was carried in a container called a powder flask or, if it was made from the horn of an animal, a powder horn. From this container the shooter poured a charge of powder into the barrel of his gun and a little into the pan for priming. Sometimes he carried the powder for priming in a separate, smaller flask. Bullets were carried in a pouch. Before going into action, a soldier frequently took a number of bullets from his pouch and put them in his mouth so that he could spit them into his gun which would be faster and easier than fumbling in his pouch each time he needed one. Also it left his hands free. At best it was a slow process since each charge of powder had to be measured and rammed home, the bullet inserted and rammed, and finally some wadding rammed on top to keep the load from rolling out.

The next step was to prepare ready measured charges of powder, and this led to cartridges. First, special nozzles were put on the flasks that would measure out a charge of powder. Then, in parts of Europe, a device called a bandolier was tried. This was a belt from which were hung a number of little tubes, each containing one charge of powder. Finally, individual charges were wrapped in paper and carried in a pouch or box. These were the first cartridges, and they appeared shortly after 1550. All the soldier had to do was tear open the paper with his teeth, spill a little powder into the pan, pour the rest down the barrel, drop in a ball, and ram the paper down on top as a wad. In these early cartridges, the balls

Powder flask of the 1600's

Powder horn

*Powder flask
of the mid-1800's*

Primer flask

*Soldier tearing off end of paper
cartridge*

were carried separately, but before 1600 methods were invented for attaching the ball to the paper-wrapped charge, and eventually it became the practice to wrap the ball inside with the powder.

Between 1830 and 1860 many different breech-loading and repeating arms were developed, and a whole group of special cartridges were invented for them. They were covered or wrapped with paper, linen, rubber, metal foils, animal tissue, and even other materials. All were still basically the same as the first paper cartridges in that they had to be set off by a spark reaching the powder from the outside through a hole in the covering. The primer which produced this spark was still separate. If the primer could be combined with the bullet and the powder, then the shooter would have only one piece of ammunition to worry about instead of two, he could carry it more easily, and he could load faster.

Leading inventors were already at work on just such a cartridge. They also wanted to make it safer and easier to handle by protecting the powder and primer with a metal case. The French made the first steps toward this goal, and produced several kinds of self-contained cartridges between 1812 and 1846. The first successful one has been called a "pinfire" cartridge. It had a regular percussion cap mounted sideways in its base. A pin was fastened right above it with one end sticking out of the side of the case.

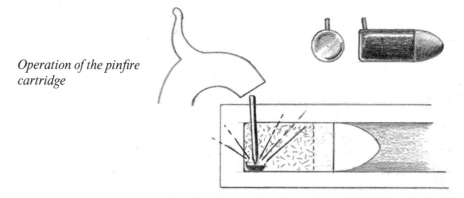

Operation of the pinfire cartridge

The gun's hammer would strike this pin and drive it into the cap and explode it. The trouble with this cartridge was that any blow on the end of the pin would set it off, and so it was a dangerous cartridge to carry around. Another cartridge had a compound of fulminate of mercury in a cavity which encircled its base rim. This was exploded by a blow from the hammer just as the percussion cap had been. In this instance, however, there was no powder in the cartridge. The fulminate of mercury also provided the charge, and it was too weak to be effective. Yet it was important because it was the first of the "rimfire" cartridges.

Two Americans, Smith and Wesson, improved upon this cartridge, added a charge of powder, and in 1858 produced the first really practical rimfire cartridge. It won quick popularity, but it, too, was soon improved

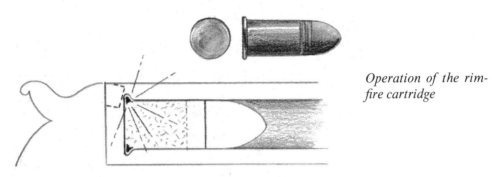

Operation of the rim-fire cartridge

upon. This time it was a cartridge with the primer in the center of the base, the so-called centerfire cartridge. Practical centerfire cartridges were made in England as early as 1852, but the final forms were perfected by Colonel Hiram Berdan of the United States, in 1866, and Colonel Edward M. Boxer of England, in 1867. There have been no major improvements since.

Centerfire cartridge

With the centerfire cartridge in a metal case, ammunition had reached a high state of perfection. No longer was it necessary to carry the bullet, the powder, and the primer separately. All were now packaged together and could be loaded with one motion instead of many. Also the metal case protected the primer and powder from accidental discharge and made them safer to carry. As a side effect, the metal case expanded when fired and formed a tight seal for the breech of the gun, finally ending the problem of gas and fire leakage that had plagued gun designers for centuries. Thus the metal cartridge ushered in the modern era of repeating firearms and made the automatic both practicable and possible.

Almost every boy is interested in firearms. There is something about a gun, old or new, that makes us want to pick it up, see how it feels, and try to work its mechanism. When this interest is properly guided, young people can benefit in many ways. From old guns they can learn history and an understanding of some of the hardships faced by the men who relied on such weapons for their lives. They can learn mechanical principles from studying gun actions. And from target practice with modern arms, they can develop physical skills that will help them in many other fields. The Department of Defense feels that such training is so important even in this age of guided missiles that it devotes much time and energy to encouraging civilian marksmanship.

But guns are not toys. They are weapons, and they must be treated with respect. Here are three rules that you should remember:

1. Never touch any gun unless there is an adult with you to show you how to handle it.

2. Always assume that any gun is loaded, even if it is a rusted relic.

3. Never point a gun at anyone. It makes no difference if it is an old gun or a new one, loaded or unloaded.

There are many more rules if you decide you want to shoot guns, but these are the basic ones for just looking.

If you are interested in actually learning how to shoot a gun, there are classes for young people with qualified teachers to show you how to do it properly and safely on special ranges where it is safe to shoot. The National Rifle Association of America considers the teaching of boys and girls one of its main purposes. It has organized clubs all over the country in summer camps, Boy Scout units, 4-H Clubs and elsewhere whenever the desire or need is found. A letter to the Association at 1600 Rhode Island Avenue, N.W., Washington 6, D. C., will bring you word on the club nearest to you and how to join it.

Largely through the work of this Association with its training and safety programs, accidents involving firearms have decreased greatly in recent years. It is fine to enjoy guns, to learn from them, and to develop skills with them, but be sure you do it properly.

INDEX